EARTH

PRACTICES

EARTH

PRACTICES

A love affair with the natural world.

Rebecca Singer

ISBN 978-1-0879-7264-0

WWW.SHAMANICENERGY.COM

BABA YAGA
PRESS

To Naomi Bob Singer,
my granddaughter,
who is new in this world.

THANK YOU

I would like to thank Wil Eadie, my husband, for encouraging me to write this book, as well as Cait Johnson and Elizabeth Cunningham (both authors) for reading the beginning of the first rough draft and reflecting that the book had a voice.

Scott Williams did a fantastic job as book designer. His creativity, care, and expertise are evident in the design,

I also want to thank Cait Johnson for her skilled editing of this book.

A huge thank you is due to Ania Aldrich whose paintings through-out the book bring the practices to life. Ania is a wonderful artist whose work is always unique regardless of the genre. It is a true honor to have her work included in this book. She is a member of TAG – www.tivoliartistsgallery.com.

Similarly, I must thank the many students over the years who have accompanied me into the wonder of the natural world to do these practices. And a special thank you to those who spoke on my behalf through testimonials.

Also, thank you so much to Gabriella Miotto, poet and doctor, and Elizabeth Cunningham (author of "The Maeve Chronicles' and much more) for their contributions of poetry. And again to Gabriella for writing the forward.

CONTENTS

Earth Practices

FOREWORD

HAVE YOU EVER SAT IN A DIFFICULT MOMENT AND WONDERED what else you could be or do to address your insomnia, your hypertension, your headache, your asthma, or any symptoms that defy naming? How your sense of wellness, in relationship with the natural world, could be expanded?

As a family physician, I find that these times come often in the exam room for me and my patients. An example:

My patient sits in silent grief, after sharing the recent deaths of his mother and brother from Covid-19. We've already addressed the diet, exercise and medications for his diabetes and hypertension. Now we turn to the Earth for help. I ask him if there is a tree in his backyard, at whose roots and trunk he might sit. He lifts his eyes, and something quickens in their gaze. Daily time with Tree has now been added to his treatment plan.

In those moments, it may occur to him that the strength of Tree's trunk against his, the roar of birdsong echoing in his bones as Sun rises, the heartbeat of the Earth heard drumming in a river's flow might shift his body's energy in such a way that he may come into greater synchrony with healing rather than disease.

I met Rebecca Singer in 2004 during her work and studies in Costa Rica, then gratefully walked the land of the Catskills in traditional teachings with her years later. Since then, I have made use of the Earth Practices that she describes so clearly, respectfully, and yes, even humorously in this book, and I have done so over and over again in all seasons. I've used them with myself, whether "Going Into Rock" in Autumn in the grief of so many Covid-19 patient deaths; or "Moon-bathing" after a long evening catching up on electronic medical records. I've shared them with my patients, teaching "Sit With Tree" to a woman with pelvic pain who is already on medications;

and "Seeing Like a Eagle" to a man suffering from hypertension and work stress. I've incorporated them into lectures and retreats with medical students and colleagues at our local university, showing them how to make Earth Practices part of a treatment plan for patients; teaching "A Heartbeat and Breath Between Earth and Sky" to help with their anxiety of trying to retain so much new material, and drumming to connect with the Earth again when so much of the day has been spent in the land of computer screens. Time and time again, I have seen how these practices in Nature bring a diminishment of pain, a clarity of thought, a deep calming. And I have also seen how they bring a joy of living in greater reciprocity with Nature, who is so generous.

May the ancient and effective Earth Practices that Rebecca Singer shares on these pages remind you that your body is a landscape, and that the natural world, with whom we are in constant relationship, offers so much wisdom for wellness and healing.

—Gabriella Miotto, MD, MPH

INTRODUCTION

ALL LIFE FORMS ON EARTH ARE OF VALUE. MY FIRST TEACHER for 13 years, Patricia Spradling, part Irish and officially adopted into the Lakota tribe, sent me to the earth to learn my lessons as a healer, and more importantly, as a full human being.

I knew I was to be a healer. When I was in my thirties, I was really in need of a teacher, and I met Patricia.

The direct experience I gained from hiking barefoot through the Cascade Mountains for 4 years, sitting with trees, watching animals for hours, learning the sounds in the rivers....all of this came into my body and helped inform my sense of belonging in the world. For 13 years I visited plants, rocks, streams, oceans, big skies, in order to better serve people as a healer/shaman.

In the three traditions that I have personally experienced—that of the Lakota people, the Costa Rican shaman near Mt.Chirripó, and the Reindeer People of Mongolia—there is a commonality. Humans are viewed as one life form, not necessarily superior in their own rite, but rather part of an interwoven ecosystem in which every element is necessary for maintaining balance.

This book is somewhat of a legacy, a call to remember that we are of the earth and do not own it, control it, or have the final say as to what life forms remain here.

Some of you are used to sitting at a desk all day and getting in your car to drive home and watch TV at night. You may take the occasional vacation to a place where are you can walk along the beach or look at a forest nearby.

Others of you may be outdoor enthusiasts who go to nature hiking, skiing, or to do another sport.

This book is an attempt to encourage you, one by one, to experience nature in a direct, profound way that will change both your view of nature and your very self. It requires that you slow down long enough to observe and soak in the natural world.

Many studies are beginning to show what native people have always known, that time spent in nature is healing. We are not meant to be glued to computers and cell phones. We are meant to walk, sometimes barefoot, to pause, slow down, breathe deeply, take in the beauty around us. To look at the tiny life forms as well as the tall trees and passing clouds. We are meant to take time to know this amazing natural world around us, be it through time spent in a city park or in the wilderness away from most humans.

These practices are very old. They are from several traditions and they are powerful. Like anything, you will get out of this book what you put into it.

I have written the practices seasonally, as this is reflected in the Medicine Wheel of many native peoples. Everything changes, everything transforms, and to witness and be a part of this ongoing shifting of energies is to be fully alive and awake.

Many of us are taught to be afraid of the natural world. In going out to do a practice, with a specific focus, you will find that the fear diminishes and is replaced with curiousity and a sense of wonder.

I have also known people who represent numerous healing modalities: doctors, chiropractors, masseurs, acupuncturists and therapists who have found these practices to be very useful for their clients.

I have had many roles in my lifetime: mother, now grandmother, wife, shaman, teacher, writer, actress, head of a nonprofit, violence prevention specialist, and musician. I am aware that I am not what I do, but who I am is found amidst the spaces between the trees in the forest. Who I am is the push to life in the springtime and the drawn-in energy of the winter.

It is my deepest hope that you will take a chance to venture into these practices, and in the process, find yourself in the reflection in a lake, the passing of a bird, or the soft feel of moss. And, in finding yourself, you will know that this earth, the natural world, is precious, interwoven and needs your stewardship, respect, and care.

SPRING

AWAKEN EARLY.

RISE DRIPPING FROM THE STREAM OF NIGHT,

WASHED WITH THE SILVER LIGHT OF MOON.

AWAKEN EARLY.

HEAR THE ROAR OF BIRD CHORUS,

SEE STARS STILL CLINGING TO STRANDS

OF AN ASHY NIGHT

—Gabriella Miotto

SPRING IS A TIME OF RENEWAL. NEW BEGINNINGS. COUR-
AGE. AN ACTIVE WILLINGNESS TO GO FORWARD, AND
THE PUSH TO LIFE THAT OCCURS IN SPRING ARE THE
EMBLEMS OF THIS SEASON.

The plans that have been incubating during the winter can come to fruition in the spring. As green shoots push through to the sun, your ideas and projects can make themselves known, become a reality.

Spring is the time to clean out unneeded belongings, as well as old tapes that loop uselessly in our minds, and beliefs that suit us no longer. Spring cleaning is both an external and internal affair.

Yes, you can clean your house and begin your garden. Yes, you can do a physical cleanse to reset your digestive health for the season.

Many of the practices for spring are more about resetting your internal world, cleaning up your emotional being, your mental state of mind, and your spirit. Beginning again is not always easy, as it requires the breaking of old habits that do not serve ourselves or others. So, here's to spring—be gentle with yourself and go forth!

5

A HEARTBEAT AND BREATH BETWEEN EARTH AND SKY

Earth Practices

A HEARTBEAT AND BREATH
BETWEEN EARTH AND SKY

FIND A PLACE OUTSIDE AS FREE FROM HUMAN AND human-made sounds as possible, where you can either sit in a chair or on a bench or on the ground, barefoot. Why barefoot? Because for this practice, you are opening your feet into the energy of the earth.

Sit so your bare feet are connected with the ground, not cross legged. If you are on the ground, this means your knees will be up. If you want to support your knees at both sides with sticks, you will be able to fully relax.

Close your eyes. Bring all of your attention to your feet. If your mind is going fast, or is loud, just let it be. You are neither going to try to stop your thoughts nor pay attention to them. Just keep bringing yourself back to the sensation of your feet on the ground.

6

After a couple of minutes, become aware of your breath. Don't change your breathing; just be aware that you *are* breathing. Now you have your awareness in two places, your feet and breath. Your eyes remain closed. You might notice that your feet are a bit warmer now.

The next focus is your heartbeat. What you are waiting for is an awareness of your pulse somewhere in your body, possibly hands, feet, legs.....some people have a difficult time with this point of attention. No worries. If you can't get it the first time, it will come gradually. Just know that your heart is beating.

Your final point of awareness is the air around your face and head. With this will come an increased attention to the sounds around you. Hopefully they are the sounds of nature.

You now have four points of awareness, with eyes still closed: feet on the earth, breath, heartbeat, and air.

Stay for a few minutes with these four points of attention. Say to yourself "I am a heartbeat and breath between Earth and Sky."

This is a profound point of self-reference, true as long as you are in a body, no matter where you are on the planet. Like a self-locating device. A good reminder at any time of day.

When you open your eyes, it is as though someone is gently lifting the eyelids. You are simply going to let in color, movement, stillness, light, shadow, form. In other words, you are not actively looking at anything, but rather letting in through your eyes. At the same time, keep your connection with your feet on the ground.

7

Everything that is happening externally is a flow of life. For these moments, there is nothing for you to do, fix, change, control. Nothing to do. Just be. Be with the energetic flow of life.

You can move your eyes. Continue to let in light, shadow, form, movement, stillness.

There is a certain vulnerability in being this passive visually. We are accustomed to "being on the lookout," to "keeping track of." Give your eyes a rest. Let your senses relax. Just Be.

Slowly, close your eyes and come back to a simple awareness of your feet on the ground.

When you are ready, open your eyes and be done.

THIS IS A PRACTICE THAT CAN BE DONE IN FIVE TO TEN minutes. If you stay with it, your body will start to long for this connection and state of being. You can gradually increase the time up to 20 minutes, taking more time in any portion of this. I would encourage you to do this daily, for five minutes.

This practice will ease stress and anxiety. Most of us carry a lot of energy mentally, with our minds leading us around like a dog on a leash. We have a hard time quieting ourselves, being receptive. When our minds are controlling all the reactions in our body, we are likely to be stressed.

First, by connecting your feet with the earth, especially if you practice this daily, you are going to start to feel a sense of being grounded, a sense of belonging.

Most people do not have this innate sense of being a part of, truly belonging here on earth. Of deep connection. This planet is our home, and yet many of us feel distant from the very ground beneath our feet. Why? Because while we walk on it, our attention is only with our racing mind.

8

Not only will this practice ease stress, it will begin to relax your abdomen. I will write at length later about the physical effects of continually holding tension in the abdomen.

For now, practice this, and know you belong. You are home. You have a right to just be. You are part of the flow of life.

The very simple fact of having your bare feet on the ground is not only good for your physical health, it's great for reminding you that you are connected to and dependent on this earth. It is also a reminder that you are not what you do. Again, you are not what you do. You are a human Being.

And you are, in essence.......a heartbeat and breath between earth and sky.

Let's talk a moment about the element of "just being" in this practice. The part where your eyes are open, you are still aware of your connection with the earth and you are letting in shapes, light, shadow, stillness, movement *with nothing to fix or change.*

These are precious moments, when we allow ourselves to just be. Our culture is very supportive of "doing." The second or third question at most social gatherings when first meeting someone is, "What do you do?" We become so identified with what we do that often our esteem is attached to that.

When we become still, receptive, and aware, we notice that everything in nature is *being.* True, a bird may be flying, a tree may be silently sending nourishment to another tree via underground roots, but these actions are an innate part of this life form's being. Not so with most of us. Many of our actions have nothing to do with our true nature.

A Heartbeat and Breath Between Earth and Sky can be a profound time to reconnect with your own nature and sense of rhythm, and to let go of having to do anything.

9

SIT WITH A TREE—FOR WOMEN

REGARDLESS OF YOUR SEXUAL PREFERENCE, IF YOU ARE IN the body of a female, begin with this tree practice, please.

Some of us appreciate trees and are aware of them as living beings. We often think of them as a lovely backdrop rather than amazing, living organisms that communicate with each other via their root systems and contain an awareness of how other trees are doing around them.

They are also wonderful models of how our own energy could be flowing within our bodies. Many different modalities address a flow of energy in our bodies as well as energy that emanates from us. Different modalities of yoga describe this, as do acupuncture and

Sit With A Tree For Women

Sit With A Tree—for Women

qui gong, all with the commonality of our energy being connected to the sky above and to the earth below.

One way of thinking of the energetic flow in your body is a hoop that extends from just below your belly button down into the earth, and another hoop from the same place, extending to the sky. These two hoops create a figure eight flowing through your body, an infinity sign, a flow of energy to earth and sky.

The hoop that flows from this point into the earth is your feminine hoop, the flow to the sky, your masculine hoop.

Sitting with a tree will help you open to the earth energy, will ground you literally and figuratively.

Women may be more comfortable doing this practice with a friend or partner who can stand watch to make sure no one or no animal (if you are in the forest) will interrupt your practice. Why? Because many women feel vulnerable in the woods alone. Furthermore, to fully immerse yourself in this practice, male or female, you must need to be not "on guard," but rather be able to relax completely.

Find a tree that you feel drawn to, either for its stature or beauty, or because it has a comfortable place for you to sit at its base. You may notice that some trees don't seem to invite visitors and others are welcoming. That is not just your imagination!

When you find your spot, sit on the ground at the base of the tree, your back to it. You may want to put a small tarp under you. Your feet are bare, or you are wearing shoes that allow you to feel the earth under you, and your knees are either resting against one another, or held in place by sticks that diagonally support them from the ground resting against the outer knee. You need to be able to relax your legs, and not have to hold them up.

Close your eyes. You are leaning against the tree, so your back is resting against it. Make any adjustments needed to be truly comfortable. You are going to sit and breathe, until your back feels melded to the tree.

Then, with your eyes still closed, with each exhale, imagine your lower body sinking into the earth. Like the roots of the tree. Imagine your pelvis opening to the earth.

Again, if your mind is busy, just let it be, and keep bringing your attention to the tree and its deep roots.

If you feel that you are going too deep, simply open your eyes for a moment. Then go back. Let yourself completely merge your lower half with this tree. Rest. Relax. Feel the energy of the earth. Feel deep into the soil, then deeper where there is warmth. Feel the fertility of the earth, the layers of energy below you. Let yourself sink into them. Let yourself rest. Keep your belly relaxed.

12

When you are ready, gently open your eyes. Consciously close off the connection into the earth. You may notice that everything seems brighter, more detailed. Your awareness has changed.

Take a moment to look around. When you rise, do it slowly. Stand with your back to the tree, making sure you are balanced and present.

Turn around and place your hands on the tree. Say thank you. Why? Because this tree being has helped you connect with earth.

YOU WILL FIND THAT THE MORE OFTEN YOU DO THIS PRACTICE, the greater sense of being connected with the earth you will have, no matter where you are. Also, your appreciation for trees will grow, as their many ways of staying rooted in all kinds of environments, their persistence in being rooted, is inspiring. You may begin to notice that trees grow out of rocks, spread their roots along mossy banks of rivers, have an amazing array of root structures and forms.

"being grounded is a physical state of being"

Being grounded is a physical state of being, not a mental one. This is key to understanding the energy flow in your own body. Imagining yourself rooted to the earth in the confines of a space indoors is not at all the same thing as sitting on the real earth with a tree.

There is energy in the earth, and this energy can become available to you with practice. The earth is forever healing and balancing herself. By sitting with a tree, and learning to go into the earth, you will build a new confidence in your walk, in your stance, and in your sense of belonging.

Sitting With a Tree will help your physical sense of balance. It will help you bring your breath into your belly and out of your chest, our natural way of breathing. This practice will reduce lower back pain, as you relax your abdomen and let your energy flow. You will also learn to relax all the organs in your abdomen. You may feel your heartbeat in your sexual organs. This can be a bit shocking if you are unused to it. Don't worry! You're alive! It's a good feeling, not one to fear.

Your legs may feel heavier after this practice because you are more grounded. If your mind has been racing, particularly over communication between yourself and someone else, this will comfort and ground you and enable you to clear your thoughts.

At first, you may feel tired after this practice. This is because you are so used to holding your energy in your mind, behind your eyes, and not being aware of what is going on in your belly, your abdomen.

13

Continuing this practice will help women open their pelvis and feel energy in the abdomen. This may be a bit scary at first. You can always open your eyes while sitting with a tree and reorient yourself.

I will go into why opening the energy in the pelvic area may be scary for women later. For now, just know that most women unconsciously do quite a bit of holding in this area. The results are many. And the letting go of this holding is the beginning of a journey to health.

SIT WITH A TREE—FOR MEN

ONE WAY OF THINKING OF THE ENERGETIC FLOW IN YOUR body is a hoop that extends from just below your belly button down into the earth, and another hoop from the same place, extending to the sky. These two hoops create a figure eight flowing through your body, an infinity sign, a flow of energy to earth and sky. The hoop that flows from this point into the earth is your feminine hoop, the flow to the sky, your masculine hoop. It is this hoop you are going to activate by sitting with a tree.

14

Find a tree that you feel drawn to, either for its stature, or beauty, or because it has a comfortable place for you to sit at its base. You may notice that some trees don't seem to invite visitors and others are welcoming. That is not just your imagination!

When you find your spot, sit on the ground at the base of the tree, your back to it. You may want to put a small tarp under you. Your feet are bare, or you are wearing shoes that allow you to feel the earth under you, and your knees are either resting against one another, or held in place by sticks that diagonally support them from the ground resting against the outer knee. You need to be able to relax your legs, and not have to hold them up.

Close your eyes. You are leaning against the tree, so your back is resting against it. Make any adjustments needed to

be truly comfortable. You are going to sit and breathe, until your back feels melded to the tree.

With your eyes closed, become aware of your spine, especially around your lower back, and then behind your heart area. You are going to connect with the energy going up to the sky, toward the sun in the tree you are sitting with. As you connect with this push upwards, you are going to imagine opening your heart area and bringing full breaths, in an easy manner, up into your chest. You are filling your chest with air, and then exhaling easily, mouth open.

You are, through the tree, connecting up into vast, spacious, clear open sky. And you are opening your heart to this vastness.

Stay with this. Maybe it will help to imagine your heart opening to the sunlight in the sky. Don't be surprised if an emotion comes to the surface.

15

If a feeling comes that is disturbing, simply open your eyes a minute, and then go back into the process. Let yourself be expansive, open, wide, clear, free, uncharted.

When you are filled with this experience, close the sky connection by placing your hands over your heart area. Open your eyes. Just sit and look around you. Everything may look brighter, as you have a heightened awareness of life. See how your heart area feels, physically and emotionally.

As a man, the sky is your place of beginning your journey to home and healing. The more you practice this going upwards through the tree, the more your breath will naturally flow first into your abdomen and then into your chest, and the deeper you will be able to breathe.

Before you stand and walk away, just place your hands on the tree trunk and thank the tree out loud. If that feels too awkward to you, then place a hand on the trunk and think "thank you."

IF YOU ENTERED THIS PRACTICE A BIT DUBIOUS ABOUT ITS benefits, I would encourage you to try this three times a week for two weeks. Your anxiety level will decrease. Your heart rate will stabilize and be slower. Your breath will be easier to send into your heart area. You may start feeling emotions that have been locked up for a long time. That is fine. If you feel overwhelmed with emotion, there are many therapists who can be helpful, or you can view your emotions like the weather. They come and go. You don't necessarily need to know why a certain feeling has come up. Just let it be, and it will pass. This is not the same as blocking it. Letting it be means that you let the tears fall, the anger be present in your body, the laughter come out.

We will talk later about having an Emotional Body. For now, enjoy the expansiveness in your chest!

16

WAKE UP WITH THE SUN!

SOME OF YOU MAY BE MORNING PEOPLE, OTHERS...NOT SO much. Even if you are one of those who awake at or before sunrise, this particular practice asks that you not be active. This is before coffee, tea, food or any activity.

Set your clock to awaken about half hour before sunrise (you can always check the sunrise time online the night before). When your alarm goes off, slowly sit up and rub your eyes. Stretch your arms gently, and as you get out of bed, be mindful that this is a new day.

Whatever your dreams, and whatever mood you awake in, please say to yourself, "This is a new day."

Waking Up With the Sun

Earth Practices

Find a comfortable place to sit, preferably outside in a chair on your lawn or porch. If not outside, go to a window that you can open and face the east.

Begin by getting centered. Sit relaxed with your feet on the grass or floor, and pay attention to your breathing. You don't need to change it in any way.

Now, with eyes open or closed, begin listening. Intently. Whether you live in the city or the country, sounds will come into your awareness. Think again, "This is a new day."

Open your eyes, and sit as the light begins to appear. Notice the smells, the changing of sounds, the coming of the light.

Notice how your body feels.

Resist the temptation to jump into action.

18

Let yourself be with the newness of this day.

Be aware of the activity, whether it be birds, cars, ocean waves, all the activity that responds to the coming of the light.

Take a moment to acknowledge the fact that the sun has its own orbit and the earth as well, and that you happen to have chosen to be at this new beginning just as the light of the sun makes itself known to you.

When there is full light, before you get up and begin the activity of your day, say to yourself one more time, "Today is a new day." You have been a witness to the coming of the day.

WHETHER YOU DO THIS ONCE IN A LIFETIME OR ONCE A WEEK, witnessing the beginning of a day is a profound experience. So many of us wake up and immediately begin the "program" of our day. We miss the amazing transition from night to day, from dark to light, from dreaming to awakening.

Every day is a new day. What we carry over from the day before, the week before, the month and year before, is, to some extent, a choice we make. I will write more about this in Seeing for the First Time. For now, notice how much more you enjoy your coffee or tea and breakfast having awakened with the light!

SEEING FOR THE FIRST TIME

FOR THIS PRACTICE, YOU WILL NEED ABOUT HALF AN HOUR
to an hour to take a slow walk.

Actually seeing and observing something is different from thinking it. For instance, as you walk along a country road, you might think, "There are a lot of trees around here." Or, your mind might simply note "trees."

This is an entirely different experience than stopping to notice the patterns in the tree bark, the smell of it, the height of it, the feel of the tree on your hand.

When we see something for the first time, our brains and bodies are in a momentarily open state, and the labels disappear so that what is happening is *direct experience.* This quality of liveliness brings us fully into the present moment.

Spring is a magical time.

When you stop and think about it, birthing is a lot of work! Imagine the tiniest green shoot having to push through layers of soil to appear above ground. There is a tremendous push to life that is happening in the spring.

Seeing For the First Time

20

Seeing For The First Time   Spring

Go outside and start by taking a walk and being conscious of the blossoms that are appearing early in spring, of the renewal of life. Look at how they are structured physically. Imagine how they know when to come up, when to unfold.

The point of going for this walk is that you see again. That you get out of your busy mind and into the moment by taking the time to explore what is around you with all your senses. Notice the quality of light, the feel of the air, the sounds around you. Be aware of colors, shapes, and even the space between things, which has its own shape. Take in the tiniest bits of moss, the forms that you usually hurry by. Be aware of your feet as you walk, of the feeling of the surface beneath you. Notice reflections of light, stillness and movement. Be aware of new growth on plants.

If you are in a city environment, walk some blocks that are not on your usual route. Take the time to look at details. Listen to the sounds. Really see people's expressions, movements. Go slowly. Look in windows and see how things are placed.

You need no destination on this walk. In fact, allowing yourself to wander is great because that encourages your ability to see as if for the first time.

When you are back from your walk, sit for a few minutes, and notice how your body feels. Curiosity is a great, powerful state of being. In fact, staying curious is essential to staying young at heart, lively, and noticing your own changes and states of mind as well.

THINK ABOUT THE SUSTAINED ENERGY REQUIRED TO GIVE birth, be it to a baby, a book, a vision, or a project. If you can tune into the push to life, you will be inspired to continue. Watch nature all spring.

Watch the growth, and the miracle of it.

The wisdom is in discerning the difference between pushing against the flow of the river and the natural push to life. It is this second energy that can propel us to action and give us the willingness to sustain our efforts whatever direction they take, especially creative efforts.

Pushing against the stream feels draining and exhausting. Following the push to life feels more like riding a wave of energy. One is definitely a forward feeling, the other not.

As you observe the rebirthing in spring, what is it in yourself that longs to come forward, that has been dormant and needs to awaken, take form?

WE HUMANS LOVE PATTERNS, PREDICTABILITY, AND SAMENESS in our environment, or at least having control over what is in our normal purview. Seeing this way will help you realize how habitual your world lens is, how much you are not present to the reality of the moment, and how much you miss! At the same time, you will be able to really relax into being with your environment by being curious about it.

This practice also introduces you to what I call your "detective mind." This state of mind can be transferred to interpersonal situations where normally you might be reactive. Instead, the possibility of closely watching and simply being curious about someone is very different from our habitual expectations of them, their behavior, and how they "should" be. Seeing for the first time implies letting go of expectations about how something or someone is, and allows us to really be present with them.

This is one of my favorite practices. I do it often, especially in places that I know well. I always find something new and different. It never ceases to amaze me that even my eyes have a certain pattern of how they take in a landscape, and the fact that the pattern skips over ground is interesting. I love the feeling of not labeling and of discovery in these walks.

SEEING LIKE AN EAGLE

IF YOU COULD CHANGE YOUR EYESIGHT FOR THAT OF AN eagle, you would see an ant crawling on the ground from the roof of a 10-story building. You would make out the expressions on a ballet dancer's face from the worst seats in the balcony without binoculars. Objects directly in your line of sight would appear magnified, and everything would be brilliantly colored, rendered in an array of shades you have never before experienced. You would also see ultraviolet light.

On top of the ability to see farther and perceive more colors, you would also have nearly double the field of view. With your eyes angled 30 degrees away from the midline of your face, you would see almost all the way behind your head with a 340-degree visual field (compared to normal humans' 180-degree field).

All this is to say that eagles have the Big Picture and the Small Picture.

23

This practice is during springtime, as the Eagle is the emblematic creature of spring according to certain North American indigenous people. We can learn from this magnificent being.

Often when we are stuck emotionally or mentally, it is because we are seeing from too close up to the situation. We are seeing out of context, not out of a larger view. Here is the practice:

Take a situation that is upsetting you, or repeatedly coming to mind.

First, sit in a quiet, uninterrupted place (preferably outside) and close your eyes. Ground yourself through your feet into the earth. Let your body relax. See if you can imagine an eagle circling high in the sky above you. Imagine its wing span, and how it might feel on the air currents.

Look at the people involved in your situation from the eagle's perspective, which is far removed, sees everyone at once, including yourself. The eagle sees you as an interconnected being. This situation is not among separate beings, but humans that affect one another in energetic exchanges.

See what part you are playing in the situation. Just watch from a distance. Observe your actions, words, reactions. Then watch everyone. Even though you can't know their thoughts, you can see their actions.

Notice what, if any, emotions are arising. Just notice them. Fear? Anger? Hope? Anxiety? Simply notice. From way up there as high as the eagle.

Imagine the eagle landing on a tree. Bring yourself back to your body. Notice how your body feels.

Did you learn anything about your part in the situation? Did you see any differences in how people were behaving? Now that you have this larger view, close your eyes again.

24

This time, you are sitting next to an eagle. An eagle is an awesome creature. Strong talons that can tear its prey apart, an enormous wing span, and the ability to harness its power, or contain its power, in a moment.

Sitting next to this being, ask for guidance in handling the situation. Simply ask with no expectations or pre-conceived answers. See what, if anything, the eagle shows you, or indicates, or what comes up in you.

In the next two days, be aware of any eagle sightings, be they a real eagle, an eagle on a book cover, a song with the word in it, or something else. Just be open. You will be surprised by how the situation resolves in you. Answers will bubble up. What, if any, actions to take will become clear.

THIS PRACTICE, LIKE ALL OF THESE IN THIS BOOK, WILL NOT work by simply reading about it. You have to take the time to do it. If you live in a place where you rarely or never see eagles, go on the internet and find a picture of one and have it there as you do this practice. You need a strong visual of an eagle to begin working. I have never known this to fail.

Eagles and spring are one and the same. It is nesting time, baby eagles are born. Adult eagles attend them. They improvise constantly according to weather conditions and babies' needs.

You may find that you too need to be open to improvising in the situation you find yourself in.

GIVE UP A STORY/SPRING CLEANING

25

WE ALL HAVE WHAT I WOULD CALL "DEFINING STORIES," poignant moments and memories that we tell over and over. Some of these serve us well, and others don't. This practice is to develop awareness about those stories that you find yourself repeating as you meet new people, converse in groups, present yourself on new occasions, are asked to "tell us about yourself" in various settings.

Sometimes we repeat stories that do not serve our well-being. Usually this is because we have not reconciled with them. We have not truly done the work of processing these events, and we tell and retell them hoping to come to peace with that moment or person.

An example would be the retelling of a time when a person really hurt you, or undermined you. A story of abuse that you have dealt with and no longer think about, but that you tell as a means of signaling, "I know what abuse is about." A story of a time when your parents mistreated you, years and years ago.

We all are a collection of stories. This practice is so that you can

Give Up A Story/Spring Cleaning

Give Up A Story/spring Cleaning

Spring

begin to be willing to give up those that no longer serve you or the ones in the story.

The first step is to become aware of a story that you would be willing to tell one last time. This is a story that you have told so many times in your life that it is, for you, part of your identity. But maybe not really in the present you. Maybe it doesn't need retelling. Maybe it could be cleaned out of your vocabulary, your psyche. Spring cleaning.

Choose one such story, and the next possible time that presents itself, go ahead and tell the story. Only before you begin, make yourself a promise. "This is the last time forever and ever that I will tell this story."

When you are back home, write a title on a small piece of paper for that story, and then burn it. Voilà! Gone! Done! You can place a big, deep, clear, lovely spring breath where that story lived in you.

TAKE THE FIRST STEP

THIS FINAL PRACTICE FOR SPRING IS ONE THAT I DEEPLY HOPE you will take to heart. Often when we are trying something new, or have a vision we want to follow, we want to see the outcome at the start!

We have also been taught that we should see the whole path in front of us when making a change. I believe this comes from the cultural norm of choosing a "career path."

The reality of transformation is that we only need to take the first step and have faith that the next step will make itself known. It does. I promise!

If you have a dream, an urge towards a new path, something you want to begin, to learn, to explore, please begin. Now is the time. You don't need to know how it will turn out.

In my experience, when we follow our hearts, life is not always easy. But if we take that first step towards a new job, a new relationship, a new place, a new frame of mind...if we take the first step, the universe provides the next. It may not look exactly like what we had in mind. So the practice is:

> Get a small plant in its baby stage the same day you begin the first step. You are going to care for this plant as it grows, as you grow with the changes you are going to make.

> Take one step (toward your project, dream, class, relationship—whatever it is).

> Stay open.

> Be willing.

> Take the next step.

> Stay open.

> Be willing.

> And watch the plant grow!

28

FOR EXAMPLE, IF YOU WANT TO TAKE A STEP TOWARDS changing your job,

Take Step One (start researching online what work might appeal to you, or begin sending in résumés, or begin networking by talking with other people who are in a field you like. Do something, and make it a daily practice.)

Stay Open By putting this energy in motion, you will come across some information that will be of interest to you, or someone may give you a name of person that would be a great resource. You need to listen and be open to exploration.

Be Willing Maybe you found a place you would like to send a resume. Go ahead, and be willing for the response. If you are getting consistent "no's" maybe you need help with your resume. Or, maybe you are under- or over-qualified. Stay with it. Be willing to put the work into this no matter if the schedule is longer than you thought.

An interesting side note here. Sometimes because we have finally built up the courage to make a change, we think it should happen quickly in our time frame. or, we think it should be simple. Everything is timing. Your personal timing has to click with that universal timing...remember how everything in nature is unfolding in the mysterious and beautiful timing of life. Your changes will unfold in their own time. Just because we have become courageous, doesn't mean everything is going to fall into place. It means you have made an important energetic shift and now you have to be open and willing to whatever it's going to take to make the changes.

Being willing might also mean being willing to live on a bit less but able to do work you truly love. Or, it may mean being willing to go back and be retrained in another field. Willing and open are two big words! Changes don't always work out the way we first imagine them.

The Next Step in your process will make itself clear. It might mean you have to take an uncomfortable risk emotionally, financially, or in some area of relationships. Change usually involves some degree of risk. You get to be the judge of the amount of risk you are willing to take.

Enjoy this time of transformation, cleansing, renewal, coming of the sun. I have heard that the sun rises with a roar. I believe it, as each new day in the spring is a day for growing.

29

May you become more aware of, connected with, and appreciative of this miracle of Mother Earth this spring. It is truly a hopeful renewal of life, filled with wonder and mystery.

Migrating birds come from thousands of miles away to return to their exact nesting places. Some mechanism allows them to remember a specific tree, yard, or bush and they hone in on it from the sky. That is truly amazing.

If you live in the country, you get to know where the nests are, when the daffodils begin to show, which trees begin to leaf out first, when to plant which vegetables in the garden.

If you live in the city, you know what streets have blossoming trees, which paths you love to bike, run, or walk. You know where your favorite springtime outdoor coffee shops are, and likely you see your surroundings shine more softly in the spring light.

A miraculous season, spring. Full of light. The return of the sun. Here's to you. May your push to life be bright and may your life blossom along with the trees and flowers. In its own time.

31

THE FALLING PETALS OF

A STAR MAGNOLIA TREE

BIRDS SINGING

DAWN AND EVENING,

COURTING AND NESTING

SPRING IS HERE

WITH ITS POWER TO

PIERCE OR BREAK HEARTS.

—Elizabeth Cunningham

SUMMER

STEEPED IN WEBS,

BRUSH,

TALL GRASSES

FIREFLIES SPARKLING

BEFORE HOT MOON

LYING IN STREAMS,

BREATH AND WATER

SUN'S LIGHT SEEPING

THROUGH BARE SKIN.

—Rebecca Singer

SUMMER. TIME TO BE OUTSIDE. A TIME OF PLAY, HEALING, AND A SEASON TO TUNE INTO THE HEALING POWERS OF THE WATER ELEMENT. TIME TO BE AWARE OF ALL THE BE-INGS THAT LOOK TO THE SUN FOR LIFE.

We are past the time of pushing to life, past the first bloom, past the rebirth into the act of living out our transformation. The prac-tices in summer are about integration, healing yourself and others. You are your own best healer. There is a great deal of energy com-ing from the sun, the earth, and the waters to offer you grace and ease during the summer.

Summer is also a time to communicate, to be part of, to gather and celebrate this earth. A time to see the plants and vegetables growing, to witness nature in its clearest light, to listen to the songbirds, see the young animals that were born in the spring. Summer is a time to go deep into water, heat, gratitude and play.

Sitting with a Tree

Earth Practices

SITTING WITH A TREE

ASSUMING YOU HAVE BEEN SITTING WITH A TREE IN THE springtime, now is the time to reverse the direction you have been working with. If you are a woman, go back and read the directions for men doing this practice. If you are a man, please read the instructions for women.

What you are going to do is complete the energetic circuit in your body going from earth to sky (women) or sky to earth (men). This is the figure eight hoop that meets about two inches below your belly button within your body.

I want to talk with you about awakening this hoop because it is powerful. A healthy flow of energy is a flow that allows a person to feel both the ground and the sky. This energetic flow also allows you to be who you came here to be, to express yourself and to be of service in a healthy way.

Also, there is a crosswise flow, between right (male) and left (female) sides of body. "Male" refers to active, present, ready to take action, logical thought, ability to speak up, congruent walk and talk, deep connection to sky, holding a big view, willing to take risks to manifest dreams.

"Female" energy refers to intuition, ability to receive, ability to "just be," awareness of cycles of the moon, connected to ceremony, deep connection to earth, creativity, and ability to feel whole emotional range.

We all have both energies if we can make them available to us, not cut off through family, culture, or spiritual blocks. Most of us need to reconnect with some part of these energies, so we then have a free flow between them, which results in good health on all levels. The earth, its elements, the animals, trees, and plants are willing to help.

It is very common for women to have lost their connection with the

38

earth. This connection is a physical, palpable sense of being rooted. Not an image, not a meditation, not a mental reality. Being rooted to the earth requires an openness in the pelvic area of women, so that there can be a flow of energy through the pelvis, down the legs, through the feet, into the earth. This is why sitting with bare feet on the earth every day is so important.

If a woman is disconnected from the earth, she will not connect with the sky hoop, or male hoop. This is why many women do not understand how men communicate, can't find their female voice, and have lost the ability to dream big. What do I mean by an energetically open pelvis?

Women have room between their organs in their abdomen. The uterus, fallopian tubes, and all sexual organs are spacious. The pelvic bone is like a rounded bowl that holds the entire area.

From our cultural upbringing, and in many cultures in innumerable ways, women are taught to be ashamed of their femaleness. We are all aware of the images of a supposedly beautiful woman...

This flat-bellied, large-breasted woman wears clothing that does not allow her to breathe, shoes that don't allow her hips to move or feet to touch the ground, keeps her beasts held in too tight bras that interfere with proper circulation. She stuffs a tampon up her vagina and runs around resenting the blood of menstruation, is unaware of the phases of the moon, and most likely fakes her non-existent orgasms.

In spite of #MeToo, the Women's Liberation Movement, and great strides in women's equality, most women still hold a great deal of shame about their bodies, don't know how to fully breathe, and one out of four have been sexually abused.

We know women have been burned, tortured, raped, and hanged for speaking up, so no wonder the throat chakra is often closed. Also, women are rarely encouraged to speak up as children. This is finally changing, but we have a loooong way to go. Greta Thunberg, current winner of the Nobel Peace Prize, is a shining example of a young woman with a working throat chakra.

Now think about a heathy flow of energy throughout a woman's pelvic region, given the cultural images, attitudes, and incredibly mixed messages about sexuality.

"the energy in the heart has to open first"

A healthy energetic flow requires an open pelvis. By "open," I am referring to a relaxed belly, where the breath first enters the abdomen, not the chest. Where both hips are able to move. Where a barefoot woman can actually feel the soles of her feet going into the earth, no matter where she is. Where the butt is not held tight, but is relaxed. Where a woman can feel her heartbeat within her cervix and/or vaginal area. A woman who, if she is still menstruating, views this as a sacred time of cleansing, and slows down for the day before and first day...maybe even stays home from work. Because she understands that, energetically, her body is cleansing any unwanted, unneeded built up energy that she has held onto that month.

40

This woman is neither constipated or suffering from diarrhea. Because she is literally and figuratively eating food that she can digest, as well as taking in the level of sensory input, information, and communication that are in balance for her system.

Best, she is able to enjoy herself as a sensual, sexual, feminine being who can feel and speak her truth.

MOST MEN ARE DISCONNECTED FROM THE SKY HOOP OF energy, which is the male hoop. Without a connection to the male hoop, they cannot connect into the earth through the female hoop.

Hence some men's disconnection and lack of respect for the earth, for women, and lack of connection with intuition and heart. And hence, some men's use of sex as a way to feel connected with the earth.

A man's lower body is solid. His whole body is solid. There is no space in the abdomen and this creates a totally different energetic pattern.

With men, the energy in the heart has to open first, a connection with the sky must be felt through the heart for energy to begin flowing in a healthy manner.

Most men are raised to talk about five things: women's bodies, sports, cars, business, and money. Men's self-worth is connected with sexual ability and money in our culture. Feelings, other than ones of power, pride, and strength, are not permitted. Feelings of fear, sadness, vulnerability are not encouraged. If a person is going to have an open heart, all feelings must be permitted.

41   A healthy man will be able to feel a wide range of emotions without fear or shame. He will have access to both logic and intuition. His shoulders will be loose because he will not be carrying the weight of the world on them. His sexuality will be an expression of intimacy or pure sexual enjoyment and never used as a weapon for power.

When a man's heart and chest are closed because of the way men are wired physically, it is easy for a man to seek sex as a way of connecting with the earth, even if temporarily. Sex becomes a means of grounding. Or a weapon, because there is a hunger to connect without the energetic means to do so.

A healthy man has a healthy appetite and good digestion because he is able to balance his need to be successful in the world with time in nature, and his definition of success will be one he has created.

He is able to walk his talk, respects women and has a profound respect for Mother Earth. He is able to take action, as well as "just be" and his protective instincts use violence only as a last resort. He is able to access both his logic and intuition.

Sitting with a Tree will go a long way in opening these energies and I would encourage you to continue this practice all summer. You will become able to sense the energetic loop within yourself into the earth and up to the sky.

LYING IN WATER

OUR BODIES ARE MOSTLY WATER. THE FLOW OF WATER IS healing and a great teacher. Water shapes the most solid of life forms over time, including rock. To lie in water is to be in the flow of cleansing energy.

Chances are the water you will be in is cold if it is early summer. Please choose a river that is relatively unpeopled. If you are fortunate enough to have access to a secluded spot where you need to wear little or no clothing, that is best. If you can't swim, wear a life vest and float on a raft.

42

Lie on your back in the river. You will have to make some effort to keep yourself afloat. Do your best to relax and concentrate on the heat of the sun. Also, be aware of the subtle rhythms of the water and the ability of the water to hold you afloat.

If you can separate your fear of being cold from the sensation of cold, you will find that your body does retain heat even in the water. Put as much concentration as possible on the heat from the sun and within your body. Relax. Keep letting go into the sensations around you and in your body.

Find a spot in the river, shallow enough that you can immerse yourself in water and be supported by rock. Close your eyes, feel the sun, and become comfortable with the flow of water over your body. Imagine with each exhale that the water is cleansing you of all illness, unease, any worries. All flowing away downstream, becoming the light on the water. Let go. Let your worries go and pay close attention to the sensations in and around your body.

When you need to, open your eyes, rest in the sun, and return to the water. Do this as often as you want.

If you will be able to relax more, do this with someone watching over you, sitting nearby, so you do not have to be alert. A guardian is great.

IT IS DIFFICULT FOR MANY OF US TO "GO WITH THE FLOW" OF our days, as we have set agendas and expectations. Inevitably, life has its own timing and rhythms, and the more we can relax into the moment, the better. Even or especially when it is not the moment we anticipated or imagined. Lying in water is a great practice to learn to release held tension and expectations and feel the literal flow of the energy of life.

Physically, letting water support you will both strengthen and soften your back muscles and help align your spine. You may find that emotions come to the surface after being in the water, the next day or even sooner.

Mentally, this practice will be a great relaxer. Our bodies were in a watery environment before birth, and we have a body memory of being supported by water. Water takes away worry, anxiety, and stress.

You will be surprised at the sense of strength you have from this practice because it brings up your resilience, your willfulness.

Most importantly this practice will give you the physical sensation of "being in the flow." Have you experienced the difference between a project that literally feels like constant pushing upstream and a proj-

ect that just seems to flow, all the pieces coming together in a relatively unstressed way? This project is in the flow.

Just as there is a magical flow of life in the natural world, many of our
human endeavors depend on timing. This is a universal timing, and
our personal timing may or may not be in tune with it. This practice
will begin to give you a sense of which of your endeavors are in the
flow or not. Then you can make a choice about whether to proceed
in spite of going against the current, or letting a project go till the
timing is right.

I am not referring to the inevitable struggles that any creative or other endeavor include. Rather, behind the whole project or attempt or
vision, there is either an energy of being timely...or not. Being conscious of either can greatly ease the frustration and create a larger
context for your efforts.

ENERGETIC CLEANSING—
FOR WOMEN ONLY

THIS IS A POWERFUL PROCESS. PLEASE HAVE SOMEONE WITH
you to stand watch, so you can take all the time you need with it. This
practice will be different each time. i recommend a repeat yearly.

**You are lying flat on the earth, sand, a rock.....within range
of a powerful water sound...a fast flowing river, a waterfall,
the ocean.**

**Wear a skirt, and take a sheet or cloth, so that you can bring
your knees up, feet on the ground, no underwear, and be
covered by the cloth. Close your eyes, and imagine opening
the top of your head to light.**

Listen to the water. When you are ready, you are going

Energetic Cleansing Near Water

to inhale the sound of the water up into your vagina, and breathe a few times while it washes around in there, and when you choose to, exhale intentionally and let everything out that wants to come out. Assume that whatever comes out is fine and will be transformed into life-giving light. You don't have to concern yourself with what to do about anything that comes out during this cleansing.

Next, when you are ready, inhale the sound of water again, and this time bring it a bit higher into your pelvic region and let it wash around for a few breaths, and again...exhale with the intention of letting everything out.

Continue doing this, bringing in the sound all the way up to your throat, bit by bit till your body is cleansed. There are areas that may need more attention than other areas.

Sometimes women experience profound grief with this, or images that are disturbing. Remember...it is a cleansing process. You are not forcing anything out. Just let it go.

When you are done, sit up slowly and feel the sun. Feel the top of your head and imagine closing the opening there. Stay at least 10 minutes just sitting and feeling the sun and your cleansed body.

MANY WOMEN HAVE HAD ABORTIONS, MISCARRIAGES, unwanted sex, less than satisfying sexual experiences, and we tend to carry the energy in our pelvic areas. This cleansing will release it. **Never do this practice close to or during your period.** It can cause life-threatening bleeding.

If, in the middle of the practice, you find yourself becoming emotional, that is fine. If you feel overwhelmed with emotion, stop, sit up, and see if you can begin again from where you left off.

The first time you do this may or may not be the strongest, most in-tense. Just know it is a way you always have of cleansing yourself inside out energetically.

The benefits of this cleansing are many. You may find, over time, that you can speak up more easily. You may feel more visible and certainly more in tune with your femininity. Your abdomen will be more relaxed and if you have uncomfortably heavy periods, they may lighten up.

MOON BATH—FOR WOMEN ONLY

THIS IS ESPECIALLY GOOD TO DO THE NIGHT OF A FULL MOON, but any night when the moon's light is accessible is good.

Bring a chair outside and simply sit under the light of the moon. Its light changes in quality at different seasons, and depending on the time of night.

First, sit with your eyes open and look directly at the moon. Then look away, and try to sense the quality of the light. Some moons are more intense than others. Is the light soft, piercing, diffused?

Now close your eyes and imagine the light of the moon bathing your body, entering your cells, informing your intu-itive self, and gently bringing light into the darker places in your psyche. Let the moon soften your heart a bit.

AS A WOMAN, YOU HAVE AN INTRICATE CONNECTION WITH the phases of the moon. Even after menopause, our bodies still "re-member" the monthly rhythms and cycles. This is why menstruat-ing is known as "moon time" among some Native American tribes. It used to be a sacred time when women did nothing but bleed and were cared for by tribal elders. Women during moon time could not be near ceremonial objects or partake of a ceremony because they themselves ARE sacred during this time and the medicine gets thrown off by their presence.

If you become attuned to the phases of the moon, your period will too, and your moon time will be at or near the full moon.

Sitting under the moon also will awaken your intuition. The moon is a powerful force, known as Grandmother Moon. Let her light guide you to listen to your intuitive knowledge and follow its lead.

LISTENING TO WATER

Go to a river or stream that flows over rocks. Find a comfortable place to sit and close your eyes. Put all of your attention on the sound of the water. If you listen carefully, you will begin to discern different tones in the water.

Focus on the lowest sounds that you hear. There will be a beat, almost like a heartbeat. See if you can hear it, and concentrate on it. At the same time, become aware of your own heartbeat somewhere in your body, not by feeling your neck with your hand, but by paying attention to the internal sensation of your heartbeat.

Stay with eyes closed, concentrated on the sound for as long as you like.

AMONG SOME NATIVE CULTURES, THIS USED TO BE THE WAY to greet a new landscape, by first acknowledging the tones in a river.

Water really is life. And rivers and streams are like the blood of a landscape. By tuning into the actual sound of the water, you will deeply relax your eyes. In fact, when you open them, after this practice, everything will appear brighter and more alive.

We spend a great deal of time looking and talking, and not enough time listening. The sound of water is the sound of life. It's the sound you heard in your mother's womb. Every stream and river has its own set of tones.

The benefit of this practice is that it is a practice of gratitude, of recognition...that you are entering a place where Water is Life and you know to take the time to recognize the flow as lifegiving. That you are humble enough to take the time to listen to the heart of the river.

LISTENING IN THE BELLY

The first few times you practice this, please be outside with your feet on the ground, with or without shoes.

There are many unspoken expectations about the way we listen to someone. We are expected to make eye contact often, and to respond with ohs and ahhs to indicate that we are hearing them. In other words, we are trained to have an external focus while listening.

This practice will allow you to hear more deeply, save your own energy, and avoid going on an emotional ride as a story is told to you. Especially powerful for empaths, this method of listening will help you stay in your own body while listening to the emotions of someone else.

The reason for being outside with your feet on the ground is that you will be able to access your belly much more easily.

Normally, when we listen, we track every word, and our energy is all up in our eyes and brain. We wonder why we are exhausted after be-

Listening to Water

ing with someone who talks a lot, and one reason is that we become ungrounded in the midst of all those words!

This type of listening is deep, and is not focused on fixing, changing, or in any way overtly responding to the person talking till they are finished, and only if they want a response. You will be surprised at how a person often solves their own issue when listened to deeply, patiently. Many of us just need to be heard. And we have a sixth sense that tells our body if we are being really attended to or not.

To begin, you connect with your feet, and become aware of your contact with the earth. Sitting comfortably, relax and place your hands in your lap, on your abdomen so you can feel your own breath gently flowing in and out of your belly.

As the person talks, you are going to stay focused on your abdomen. You may not hear every single word, that is fine. You do not need to maintain eye contact, and you do not need to signal that you are listening other than to nod your head now and then. No matter how emotional the person's story is, you are going to stay in your belly and listen.

THE SURPRISING NEWS IS THAT, BY DOING THIS, YOU WILL have heard the true emotional story being told. It is a kind of witnessing. And the person will know they have been heard. And the next best news is that you will not be tired, drained, or feel pulled out of your own being.

You will not get caught up in the emotions of the person's experience yourself. This does not make you less compassionate or caring. In fact, it allows you to hear more clearly and respond in a more helpful way.

This really takes practice. It goes against many of our cultural norms about listening. When, and only when, you are comfortable and able to do this outside with your feet on the ground, bring the practice inside.

51

The benefits are many. Other people often drain us without our being aware of it. You may walk away from an interaction and feel either filled or drained. We are in a continual exchange of energy with one another. The issue, in this culture, is that we are expected to be extroverted at all times. It is exhausting.

You will be able to interact with people and maintain your own energetic state. In addition, if a person is having a hard time, you don't need to go on the roller coaster with them. If you are in a job where people are constantly complaining, you will feel so much better at the end of your work day!

This practice also definitely affects digestion for the better. We digest food, but we also digest words! If you don't have to take in every word that is being said to you, but can remain centered and in your body, your stomach will be much happier. Your anxiety level will decrease, and you will learn to "stay with yourself."

52

NIGHT WALK

THIS PRACTICE IS BEST DONE SOMEWHERE AWAY FROM street lights. A forest is best, or near the ocean. You want the only sources of light to be natural, like the moon, or snow, or (if you are in the rainforest) bugs that light up and mushrooms that glow in the dark. It's true!

We have a healthy fear of the dark on an animal, survival level in our bodies. We also have a very unhealthy fear of the dark based on cultural teachings, the 24/7 news cycle, and endless movies equating the dark with danger.

Learning to walk at night is an invaluable practice. At first, take a headlight, and turn it on as you feel the need, and do this practice with a companion. When you begin this practice, the moon should be at least half full.

The first step is to use your feet as your eyes. If you are walking on a trail in the woods, let your feet feel their way along. Go as slowly as you need to. Keep telling your body to relax. Listen to the sounds. If you are at the ocean, listen to the rhythm of the waves.

think or say "in this moment... I am safe."

Once your eyes become accustomed to the dark, you will be amazed at the amount of light that is present in the natural world at night. The moonlight will give certain plants an iridescent quality. Any white blossom will stand out.

Let your mind run through all the scary possibilities...animals, humans, whatever you fear will come up. Begin a walking meditation...on the in breath think or say... "In this moment" and on the outbreath, "I am safe." Keep going for awhile with this thought and stay relaxed.

Most animals are more afraid of you then you are of them. Let unexpected noises be. Keep going at a pace that is comfortable and try not using your headlight at all. If you are stepping over fallen branches or logs, give some space before you step on them, and also as you step off, as snakes like to sleep near them in some areas of the country.

What you will begin to experience is that night time is somewhat magical and wonderful, peaceful and only different from day time. Not safer or scarier, just different. This is a whole aspect of life you have likely been missing out on, and one that I hope will become a part of your life now and then.

WALKING AT NIGHT HAS SO MANY BENEFITS. YOU CAN TEACH your nervous system to be on alert in a relaxed way as opposed to a "high alert" that causes tension. Your eyes get a rest if you let your feet do the seeing. Your sense of trust and well-being will be heightened as you find comfort rather than fear in nighttime.

You will be amazed at the brightness and amount of artificial light we have come to use as "normal" and "necessary." In fact, walking at night can actually improve your eyesight, as you learn to strain less. Your balance will also improve from night walking, as will your blood pressure levels. Your curiosity will be awakened. And last, but not least, you will sleep better once you know the night. That is quite a bit of benefit from one practice!

BOUNDARIES

IN ORDER TO BE OF SERVICE TO OTHERS, WE NEED TO CARE for ourselves first. I am going to say that again as it bears repeating. In order to be of service to others we need to care for ourselves first.

This self-care can be summed up in one word: boundaries. A boundary is a clear delineation between self and other. There are innumerable reasons why people have trouble setting boundaries. Guilt, poor modeling in the family of origin, lack of self-esteem...the list goes on and on. However, if you watch most animals in nature, they are great at setting boundaries.

Have you ever seen one animal signaling "no" to another animal in any way? This may take the form of a growl, a snarl, or a pounce! Animals have a magnificent variety of ways to set boundaries and it usually involves signaling, "No....no farther, no you cannot have my food, no I don't want to play, no I am sleeping, no you cannot come onto my turf."

As odd as this first practice may sound, it is the first step in feeling your boundaries on the physical plane. You will be surprised how often you are unaware of your physical self once you begin to practice this first boundary setting.

BODY BOUNDARY

Simply go for a walk on a fairly uncrowded path or road. As you walk, be aware of all the outside of your body, the outmost layer of skin both in your front and back body. Keep bringing your awareness back to this outer layer that signifies your body.

Feel the breeze or heat on your skin. Feel the soles of your feet in your shoes. Your back, neck, back of your head. See if you can sense the entire area of your body while you walk.

Come to a place where you can stand still. Continue being aware of your entire body surface. Be aware of temperature change, movement of air. Contraction or expansion. This is your body boundary.

Try staying aware of your body boundary throughout the day. Check in now and then.

The benefit of this will be surprising. You will begin to notice when you feel that someone is "in your space." This is because not only do we have a physical body boundary, we have an energetic one that extends out past our physical selves. How far depends on your mood, your awareness of your own energy, and your ability to draw in or spread out your energy.

For now, just be aware of when someone feels too close, and adjust yourself. You may need to turn slightly away, or step to the side. You can do this discretely. Keep checking in throughout the day and see how your body feels in relation to how close or far someone or a group is from you. See if you can obey your body boundaries so that you stay comfortable.

If someone is too close, you are likely to tense up, even hold your breath. Your body will be trying to withdraw to what feels like a comfortable distance even though you aren't moving, and this is what causes the tension. See if you can give yourself permission to take care of your body's signals and adjust. It takes practice!

THE BENEFITS OF THIS ARE RATHER SURPRISING. MUCH OF the tension we come home with every day is a result of not listening to our body's signals around boundary comfort. It is OK to back up. It is OK to move to the side. Your comfort level is going to shift around different people.

If you start listening and acting on behalf of your physical boundaries, you will feel considerably less drained. Your stomach will relax, and you will have less muscular soreness from "holding" your own body together when there is no need.

Also, your level of general tension will decrease, as you literally give yourself room to breathe and feel and occupy your body!

56

STAND IN A STREAM OR RIVER

AS A FINAL PRACTICE FOR SUMMER, STANDING IN A STREAM or river (your choice) can physicalize how you approach both projects and relationships.

At different times in our lives, we feel more ambivalent about "going against the flow," or struggling to make something happen. What may be perceived as a wonderful challenge in our 30s can feel like a waste of energy 10 years later. This practice is like a small test for how you are really feeling about a project, a relationship, or a new idea.

Find a stream or river with a current strong enough that you have to use some leg muscle to stay balanced. Stand in the

Stand in a Stream or River

Earth Practices

direction of the flow, close your eyes, and let your body experience that energy, the force of the water, and the pace of the flow. Stand a few minutes this way, opening your eyes for a few moments when you need to.

Then, very slowly, turn so that you are standing against the flow. Find your balance, and again... close your eyes and become aware of the effort this takes in your body. Just stay, and be aware of the sensation of being in this direction... against the flow.

Ask yourself, do you have the desire and willingness to make the effort it takes to stand against the flow and walk upstream?

Ask yourself, are you willing to wait till what is needed finds you while you stand in the flow?

Without judgement, acknowledging your energy, this practice can help you decide whether to begin, stay in, or end an endeavor. It is like taking your own temperature.

SUMMER IS A TIME FOR HEALING, PLAYING, TUNING INTO THE watery world. A time of expression, opening your heart, and welcoming the heat and sun. Nature is in its full expression—not withholding—and you are invited to join in.

Summer is time to speak your truth, be fully who you are, and breathe deeply, rest, be lazy, play, let go, and come to fruition. Be who you came here to be.

59

Earth Practices

WHO I MET
TODAY ON MY WALK

RAIN-ON-FACE,

EARTHWORM-IN-CREEK,

CROW-ON-BRANCH,

WIND-IN-HAIR.

60

—Gabriella Miotto

AUTUMN

SEE THE ACORN,

THE WHOLE TREE HELD WITHIN

FALLING TO EARTH

THROUGH ANCIENT AUTUMN LIGHT

TILL THREE HUNDRED

SPIRALING CIRCLES SPIN.

—Elizabeth Cunningham

A UTUMN IS SUCH A WONDERFUL TEACHER. IT'S THE SEASON OF TRANSFORMATION, THE BEGINNING OF GOING DEEPLY INWARD, AND A TIME TO LEARN TO BE IN THE MOMENT.

Autumn is our bridge between the light of summer and the dark of winter, the fullness of life in summer and the quiet of winter. Autumn is the "in between" time when we are in the midst of transformation.

Every living thing is always in this process, but autumn brings change to us in a way we can't hide from, and with great beauty. Every living thing must die; autumn is a great teacher in how to let go, when to let go, and the biggest "letting go" of all: death.

Many people who live in climates with severe winters miss autumn's magical teachings because they anticipate the coming cold hardship of winter and so miss the moment of being with autumn. This is what leads me to begin with Being in the Moment.

BEING IN THE MOMENT/
DAILY AUTUMN WALK

FROM THE TIME THE SUMMER LIGHT BEGINS TO SHIFT, AND the air as well, autumn introduces itself to us subtly, then more blatantly as the leaves shift into glorious patterns of color.

This practice is about being with Autumn, from beginning to end. It is a daily practice of a 20-minute walk at the same time (of your choice) every day. I recommend walking when the shifting of the light is most noticeable. As you are walking, simply note the quality of the light. Also be aware of a difference in the air, a slight coolness, the smallest chill. Take a walk at the same time every day (as long as weather permits) and be aware of the what is going on around you with the light, air, and the leaves of the trees.

66

Be in the moment, be present. Notice how people are dressing differently. If you are near a park, or live in the countryside, be aware of the harvest of autumn. What is changing in your diet? What options do you have now that it is harvest time?

What are the animals doing differently? Are there birds that are preparing to leave, or have already begun their migrations? Are certain flowers drying up, becoming brown? Going on the same walk at the same time every day, you are going to get to know a small bit of your world intimately and follow it through the season of transition.

Look both at the big picture of light and air, and at details. Do you notice webs where there were none? Is something blossoming or dying? Do the windows in a city change to "autumn" displays? Be aware of the changes. The transitions.

THE DAYS ARE BECOMING SHORTER, AND IF YOU KEEP THIS daily practice, the same walk at the same time, you will be acutely aware of the shortening of the day as well as the beauty of this season. It is an ever-changing beauty that cannot be captured, stopped, caught, or controlled. Autumn is a great teacher about the constancy of change. See if you can walk in it, with it, enjoy it, and be in the moment. Summer is over and winter is not yet here. Rest in the transformation.

The more you can accept that everything changes constantly, the less anxious you will be. The more present you are in the moment, the less anxious you will be. Stay with yourself. Stay with your body, your emotions, your thoughts in this moment. They will pass. Everything does. Don't miss out on your life by being in the past or the future. Your body will relax. Your mind will be clearer, and your spirit present.

GOING INTO ROCK

MOST OF US THINK OF ROCKS AS THINGS, NOT BEINGS. I experience rocks as very much alive and full of energy, and larger rocks as an accumulation and manifestation of passing time. Rocks stay when many natural materials do not. Rocks can be millions of years old.

Most of us also think of rocks as hard surfaces, unmoving and still. This practice is to introduce you to the great comfort, grounded being, and wisdom of rock.

Autumn is a preparation for a much more internal time. Rocks can introduce you to going inward in a comforting and surprising way.

You will need a place where there are rocks big enough to comfortably lie on. Big enough that your whole body can

be stretched out or comfortably curled up on the surface of the rock. It is up to you if the rock is in the sun or shade, next to water or not. Wherever it is, you need to be able to get as comfortable as possible lying down on your front, back, or side and completely relaxing into the rock.

At first, you will be acutely aware of the rock's hardness, and its seemingly ungiving surface. As you relax your own muscles and give in to the rock, the sense of where your body stops and where the rock starts will become less clear. Close your eyes, and allow yourself to be completely relaxed, as if you were going to sleep. (If you do sleep, that is fine!)

You will slowly realize that the rock no longer feels either hard or completely still. A deep sense of movement within the rock is likely to make itself known to you, and the surface is likely to feel quite comforting.

The comfort is partially physical but also emotional. You can depend on this rock through a transitional time, both through a changing season and through changes within yourself. The expression "S/he is my rock" comes from this quality of a form of life that, although it does transform, changes so slowly that we don't perceive those changes in a lifetime.

FIND YOURSELF A ROCK YOU CAN GO TO, AND GO INTO. YOUR autumn rock. What is it in you that remains constant through all the changes of autumn? A good question to ask before lying down and contemplating while resting deep in rock.

Getting to know a big rock is like making a friend for life. The benefits of knowing there is a seemingly hard, immobile surface that is actually soft and strong, sturdy and dependable is a great comfort.

THE AUTUMN BASKET

IF YOU HAVE BEEN PAYING ATTENTION TO THE SEASONS, YOU have noticed by now that there is an exquisite timing in this world. That every life form comes into being when the conditions are best for it to thrive and that in nature there is a harmonious timing to everything.

Our own personal desires to want things to happen or to create something may or may not be in alignment with this universal timing. Things tend to work out better when they are well timed. You can see this in examples of people who come forward with ideas, books, music, creative endeavors that we think of as "timely." However, most of us want what we want when we want it, and that often means Now!

This practice of making an Autumn Basket is for you to get a sense of what it is like to combine your deep wishes and to align them with universal timing, that magical timing which is so prevalent in nature.

Find a small basket, maybe large enough for 5 apples. You are going to fill it with autumn leaves. It doesn't matter if the leaves are newly fallen or getting dry and wilted.

To this basket of leaves you are going to add three small, thin pieces of paper. On each paper you have one wish. These wishes are things you really want to have happen in your life or in someone's life. You are going to crumple each strip of paper up and mix it in with the leaves and hang the basket somewhere visible. Throughout the autumn, as you look at this basket, you may have the thought that you want to align your personal timing with universal timing. It is a matter of learning and trusting that timing is essential to materializing your wishes.

At the end of autumn, burn the contents of the basket and

Letting Go

The Autumn Basket

Autumn

use it again next autumn. Maybe keep a journal about when the three things come into being, and how the timing is right, even though something may happen faster or slower than you had in mind.

LETTING GO

WHETHER IT'S A POSSESSION, A QUALITY IN OURSELVES, A fear we want to be over and done with, or a friendship that has reached its end, letting go is something we often struggle with.

Trees in the autumn are the perfect teachers. The trees don't wiggle and shake in an effort to get leaves to fall. Neither do they curl in their branches and refuse to let go of them. Each leaf falls from a tree with grace, when the conditions and time are right. It is without push-pull, struggle, or complicated maneuvering.

71

Spend some time outside in a place where you can sit quietly and observe the leaves falling. Each has its own path to the ground, often spiraling or moving along the route of a breeze till it lands on the earth. What a graceful, peaceful letting go.

WE DO NOT LET GO OF HABITS, EVEN VERY DESTRUCTIVE ONES, till we are ready. No amount of cajoling or advice can get us ready. We may have a few failed starts, but there will come a time when, like the tree, we are ready to let go...and no one can push us to be ready. We can do the work to be willing...but letting go of a relationship, a possession, a habit, a response, a way of being...take the tree as your teacher. There is a season for letting go. There is a time to let go. Take the pressure off yourself and let yourself feel when the timing is right.

GATHERING BOUQUET

PART OF THE BEAUTY OF AUTUMN IS THAT THE SEASON HOLDS both "letting go" and gathering. This is the time we harvest what has grown over the summer, as well as the time we begin to prepare for what we will need for winter.

To gather your bouquet, which you are going to place in a large vase or dish, with or without water, you will need to go to the woods, or at least a park. You may be able to gather much of what you need from your own yard, especially if there are dying flowers, grasses, and branches.

This bouquet is made of dried, once blooming life. Of flowers that are past their time, grasses that have gone the color of wheat, and blossoms that are brown and withered.

The purpose of this gathering is to see the beauty in the death of these forms of life. To honor the dying that is part of autumn. To find wonder in what is left after the life is gone.

You may initially think that you wouldn't want something so ugly in your home. But I can almost surely promise you that rather than being a depressing sight, this bouquet will awaken a new appreciation for the process of dying. There is beauty in the array of browns, the shapes, the forms. Arrange a bouquet that is pleasing to you in shape and form. Live with it for a couple of weeks.

THERE IS A WAY AND A TIME, EVEN IN HUMAN LIFE, WHERE the lines between life and death seem to intermingle. In the last breaths that a person takes, no matter how peaceful or grasping, life and death are a mix. And after the last breath, the air is still full of the life of that person.

This bouquet may help you realize that death is a part of living, not the linear end in a line, but part of the circular cycle of the seasons.

GATHER AND LET GO

THIS IS A PERFECT METAPHOR FOR WHAT IS HAPPENING IN autumn. For this practice, you will need a small backpack.

Go outside a collect a rock for every worry and fear you are carrying around. Make sure each rock is no larger than the palm of your hand. Know what each rock represents as you collect it and place it in your backpack.

This collecting does not have to happen all at once. You may become aware of more worries and fears that you burden yourself with on a daily basis. Get a rock for each one.

When you have collected them all, and they are all in your backpack, you are going to go for an autumn walk that will end either at a stream, river, lake, or large pond. You need to walk at least 20 minutes with this back pack on your back, and be aware of the worries and fears that are represented in there.

When you arrive at your destination, find some privacy, and one by one, toss the rocks into the water. You might not remember which rock is representing what fear or worry. It is not important to know. Just consciously throw each one into the water, till your pack is empty.

Then turn around, put your pack on your back and walk to your starting point. Be aware of the difference when you are not carrying the weight of those rocks!

73

Gather and Let Go

I DO NOT BELIEVE WE CAN SIMPLY "LET GO" OF FEARS AND worries. But I do think it is beneficial to be aware of the toll they take on our bodies and spirits.

Maybe during autumn you could decide to do your best not to focus on a few of them as you go into winter. Maybe you could make a conscious decision to turn your attention elsewhere when a habitual worry arises.

This practice could be done in any season, but I think it is most suited to autumn, time of change and transition.

LET IT FLOW LET IT GO

Find a beautiful stream or river, some water source that flows and allows you to lie near it comfortably. Lying down on a blanket is preferable to sitting, so you can really relax.

Become aware of the sound of the flowing water, and keep bringing your attention to it. Hopefully you are also somewhere near trees that are in full autumn color, but if not, the stream or river is fine.

Our thoughts arise and flow, unless we fixate on them. Once you have become as relaxed as possible, head to toe, listening to the flow of water, you are going to observe your thoughts.

Just breathe in and out naturally, and be aware of the flow of your thoughts. Be aware of the spaces between thoughts. Stay with this practice. After awhile, tell yourself that this flow of thoughts is "mental energy." You can pay attention to it, be led around by it, or just let it flow. Not trying to stop your thought process and not getting caught up in it. Just like the river, flowing.

Open your eyes, sit up slowly and see if you can continue to experience your thoughts as mental energy as you watch the river or stream. A flow.

IF YOU CAN STAY WITH THIS, begin to look around at the trees and with soft eyes, let in the light, the color, the air, the sounds. Let it in and let it flow, like the water.

By now, hopefully you are feeling very relaxed and receptive. You have transitioned from "trying to keep track of" to noticing the flow.

"be aware of the spaces between thoughts."

Imagine taking this practice inside to your work, the grocery store, to your life at home. Watching and letting it flow. Being a part of the flow.

This practice is best begun in the fall, when all is flowing toward change, shift, and rest.

76

A SMALL DEATH

YOU MAY FIND THIS PRACTICE WORKS BETTER FOR YOU IF someone accompanies you and reads it to you slowly. But it is just as possible to do it on your own, first reading it and then lying down and following the practice.

Death is a great teacher. In many cultures, death is talked about, is physically represented in daily life. The skeletons that take every form in Mexican culture, the Day of the Dead, and celebrations of ancestors are common around the world.

In our culture, we often avoid the subject unless someone we know is dying, and we certainly don't like contemplating our own deaths. However, what better way to access how you are living your life than to look at it through the lens of dying or being dead. What a great way to get perspective on what is really important, and to evaluate if you are on a path that feels good to you, meaningful.

It is inevitable. We all die. That leaves the question, how do we want to be living? And when we die and look back at our lives, how do we want to feel and what needs to shift in order to die without big regrets, things left unsaid or undone?

Go to a river or anywhere within reach of the sound of water. It could be the ocean, a stream, on a porch during a rain.

Be in a comfortable position, sitting or lying down. Close your eyes.

Imagine yourself floating on a slow-moving river in the sun-light. It takes very little effort to stay afloat, and you relax your body with the support of the water. You can feel the small waves and ripples of water beneath your body, and you can feel the warm sun on your face. You are alone and safe. Alone and safe.

You let your body gently float and with very little effort, you relax more into the support of the water.

At some point, with ease, you take your consciousness up to a cliff above the water and see yourself down there, float-ing. You can see your body on the river, the sunlight on your body, and the movement of the water.

Again with ease, you are going to watch your body dis-integrate until you are only a skeleton on the water. Your bones remain in place. You can see your skull, spine, all of the bones of your body in place. They may or may not begin drifting apart. Either way is fine; you just watch them. Your body is gone, mind is gone. You are nothing but bones on the water. Just watch. Observe.

At some point, you are going to gather your bones into place if they have drifted simply by directing or asking them to come together. There is your complete skeleton. Now you are going to begin filling in your body with muscle, organs, blood-flow. Don't worry, you don't have to remember everything. Your body will fill itself in till there you are, complete and whole, once again floating on the water.

With no hesitation, your consciousness enters your body on the water. Again, you can feel the water supporting you and the sunlight. Relaxed. Relaxed.

Slowly you are going to bring your awareness back to your true body lying on the blanket or sitting where you are. Scan your body, head to toe, to feel every inch of yourself from the inside out.

Slowly open your eyes and bring yourself completely back to the present. Take a moment to stretch.

HOW DID THIS MEDITATION MAKE YOU FEEL? DID YOU LIKE seeing yourself as a skeleton? Was it too scary to imagine? Might you need to do this in steps till you are able to look at yourself as bones?

This autumn Small Death practice can be a powerful one to integrate. The effect of the meditation may not be immediate. Don't be surprised if something comes to you a week later regarding your life.

Autumn is a time of dying. Wouldn't life be more easily lived without fear of death? Wouldn't conversation be more relaxed if the subject of death could be included without it being so charged? Death is not the end of life. Death is a part of life. Autumn is our best teacher.

My hope is that you come to love this season of change. Autumn full moon is glorious. The colors, the shift of light. What a magical, miraculous season. Don't miss it! Be present. Watch the leaves fall, each finding its own path to the earth. Listen to the changes in bird-song, the rain, the way the light has softened. Feel the chill in the air towards the end of autumn, the shortening of the days, the slowly increasing feeling of wanting to enjoy a warm winter home.

79

IT IS ALL POETRY,

EVEN A DARK MORNING

AT THE END OF FALL,

TWISTING OAK

BRANCHES REVEALED,

SMALL BIRDS AND

THE LAST LACY LEAVES

STILL HOLDING FAST

—Elizabeth Cunningham

WINTER

MEETING BUFFALO

BUFFALO SLOWLY RISES

SHAKES SNOW FROM HIS MASSIVE BACK

AND APPROACHES ME

ON THIS NEVER-ENDING WINTER PRAIRIE.

HE STANDS SO CLOSE,

I SMELL GRASS ON HIS BREATH

HEAR THE DRUM OF HIS HEART

FEEL THE FIRE IN HIS BODY.

I WANT TO BE REWILDED.

—Gabriella Miotto

WHAT A CHANGE! THE LEAVES HAVE FALLEN OFF THE DECIDUOUS TREES, THE TEMPERATURE CONTINUES TO FALL. THE DAYS ARE GETTING SHORTER, AND THE WEATHER MORE UNPREDICTABLE. THE LIGHT IS TOTALLY DIFFERENT, ON THE ONE HAND MUTED, ON THE OTHER SO BRIGHT ON SUNNY DAYS WHEN SNOW IS ON THE GROUND.

Every other creature besides humans knows to slow down in the winter, knows that winter is a dormant time, a time to regroup, dream, recharge by resting, and spend more time simply being.

Modern life does not allow us this change, nor would many of us choose it, since we are so accustomed and perhaps attached to going from one thing to another. Few jobs allow people a change in tempo just because it's winter. And the holiday season ramps everyone up from Halloween through New Year's, sending the majority on shopping sprees, involving traffic jams, crowds, and stress.

These winter practices encourage you to slow down when and where you can, with the understanding that in today's world this change of rhythm may be challenging.

Part of the work of winter is discovering what faith is for you. Is it a set of philosophical rules that you turn to in times of abundance and stress? Is faith an attitude? Is it the ability to put one foot in front of the other when you can't see further than your next step? Is faith the willingness to participate in all of Life's aspects? What is it for **you**?

The symbol of faith in many native tribes is the Buffalo, guardian of the North Gate. The buffalo always faces the storm, head down, and endures, knowing it will pass. The buffalo embodies a willingness to be determined in the face of whatever life serves up.

Another symbol of deep faith is the mama polar bear, who gives birth while half asleep and trusts that her cubs will find their way to her milk supply. Imagine that.

More than any other time, winter holds the possibility for sudden shifts. The unexpected. It is important to get quiet inside, deeply so...and listen to the north winds and let in the stream of light from the North.

85

YOU WILL NEED WARM WINTER CLOTHING BECAUSE THESE practices are outside, as in every season. It is possible to be very comfortable and warm in even harsh winter weather if you can invest in a few warm essentials. Often thrift stores have great winter clothing if you can't invest in brand new.

We will begin with a practice that will make all other winter practices more comfortable for you.

THE WARMING BREATH

MANY OF US THINK ON A WINTRY DAY, "I CAN'T GO OUT THERE. It's too cold." Although on some days when frostbite is possible, this is true, on most winter days in most of the country going outside is safe and possible. You may not feel like going out, but you can.

Many people have cold and fear mixed up together. On a primal level, cold is dangerous for survival. If we have had experiences of being left in the cold, or not cared for as children when it was cold, our bodies remember. Cold and unsafe become one in our body.

This is the season of sudden change, breath, a different light, and great faith. This is the season that allows us to withstand the difficulties and pain of life and celebrate the joys and wonders. It is in the time of winter when we gather in celebrations of light, to bring light into the darkness.

Sometimes, for some people and animals, winter is a time of death. There is not enough food. Other times people freeze to death, or do not get the help they need with illnesses. Winters are a time of great patience.

The first step in The Warming Breath is to dress warmly enough that you can go for a walk on a winter day and be warm.

The Warming Breath

Earth Practices

When you are dressed and ready to go out, you are going to begin by relaxing all your muscles. As you start to go on your walk, you are going to come back to your body often and remind yourself to relax. Tensing and bracing against the cold only makes you colder!

I suggest you try the following before going for a walk. Try it in the comfort of your home till the imagery is working for you.

Imagine a coal in your belly, deep inside, about two inches below your navel and in between your abdomen and spine. This is a coal that is lit.

On the inbreath you are going to focus on heating up the coal. Imagine it coming to life with fire, heat, an orange-red glow. On the exhale, you are going to imagine this heat spreading out through your entire body.

Spend a few five-minute breathing sessions with this imagery before you venture out for your first Warming Breath walk.

Now that you are dressed warmly and have reminded your-self to relax your muscles as you walk, and have practiced the breath and images....you are ready for your winter walk!

Pick a day that is not a major challenge for you. Just like learning to drive in a snowstorm is not ideal, learning to re-ally relax and BE with winter on a walk needs to be learned in conditions that are possible for you. So pick a day when you normally would stay in and venture out.

As you walk, continue to check in and remind your body to relax. Relax your forehead, your eyes, your jaw, neck, shoulders, chest, back, belly, hips, legs, feet. Relax.

Begin the warming breath as soon as possible, once you have established a walking rhythm. Inhale, imagining the coal brightening; exhale heat throughout your body. It will take awhile before you are able to both do this breath and notice what is going on around you, but not long. The breath will become automatic, and then you can begin to enjoy the beauty around you.

Just go out for 10 to 15 minutes at first. You can extend this time indefinitely. I am often out for hours in the winter, and I always return to this practice when I need it to get warm and stay warm.

THE BENEFITS YOU RECEIVE FROM BEING OUT IN THE WINTER are many. First, you become aware of the incredible beauty of the season. You may have in your mind that winter is stark, without color, and everything is dead. That is just not true. There are muted colors, an array of golds, brown, reds, purples, depending on where you live. A bright blue winter sky is such a treat! And many birds stay the winter and are particularly beautiful seen against a snowy branch.

Although plants and flowers do die in the winter, the majority of life forms go dormant, which is altogether different. Bears hibernate. Snakes go underground. Deer go deep into the woods and hunker down together. Trees store energy, communicating through their root systems. Beneath the earth's surface, a lot of life is quietly preparing itself for rest and rebirth.

YOUR OWN SONG

FOR THOSE OF YOU UNUSED TO SINGING, THIS PRACTICE WILL be a bit new! I use the word "song" here loosely, meaning anything from a gentle hum, to a melody with or without words, to a full-blown howl!

The best time for this practice is right after a newly fallen snow. However, if you live in a winter without snow, find a quiet day and go

Your Own Song

somewhere that you feel comfortable making sounds, outside. Possibly by the ocean, in the woods, at a lake, a public park.

Begin by letting out a sound as you exhale. Like an "ahh" or "uhhh." A small sound. Then look around you, and either walking or being still, start humming to the trees, the ocean, whatever nature is around you. Hum as though they can hear you, as if you are humming To them and For them.

You may feel silly at first, but keep going. See if any words want to accompany your humming. Please do your best to get your logical and self-critical mind to leave you alone! Maybe one word will come to you, maybe several.

See if you make a song, your personal song, to the winter. You can sing to the sky, the winter light, the dark, the cold, the wind, the snow, the air, any aspect of the season.

91

If you are feeling like a child, the practice is working!

As you go about your day, bring whatever humming or song for winter that has come, include it while you are driving, doing laundry, cooking. Like a comforting tune to accompany you in this season.

Your song can change and develop as the season goes on.

THE BENEFITS OF THIS PRACTICE ARE THE COMFORT THAT IT will bring to you on a deep level, the recognition of all living beings this season, and the sound of your own voice being let into the world in a nonedited way.

Surprisingly, if you are prone to sore throats, you will get fewer with this practice. Opening the throat and allowing breath and tone at the same time is a release of often held energy. You may be surprised at what wants out!

HEALING WINTER LIGHT

I BELIEVE THIS IS ONE OF THE MOST IMPORTANT PRACTICES in this book. The light that is available in winter is truly remarkable, and will be a great force for your well-being, envisioning, and imagination.

If possible, go for a walk on a sunny day to a place where there are icicles. Ideally this is at a river, but you can find icicles hanging off a roof, garage, or any number of places. The idea is to see the winter light in the icicle.

There is a quality of bright, cool, "captured" or "focused" light in the icicles. This is the Healing Winter Light. This is the light that you will be bringing to mind in the next practice, which is a meditation. It is very similar to the light in very clear quartz crystals when held up to the sun.

If you have no access to icicles, then look at them online, and carefully notice the light within them. See if you can find that light anywhere in the landscape of your present living circumstances. Even an ice cube under the light has this quality.

92

When you have a clear experience of this light, find a quiet, warm, comfortable place inside to sit. Make sure you will not be interrupted. Close your eyes and relax your body. Imagine this light entering in a soft, steady flow through the crown of your head.

Or, if you prefer, imagine it entering through your third eye. This is the space between the inner edge of your eyebrows. You can imagine a shaft of Northern light coming into you, and creating a deep trust in your intuition and ability to know what is right for you.

THE WINTER IS THE TIME TO STRENGTHEN YOUR RELATIONSHIP
with your intuition, as this will serve you well in all seasons.

have a "go to" internal safe place

I would encourage you to work with this light throughout the winter. This practice has some unexpected results. If you have headaches, they should significantly decrease. Your dreams may be both more vivid and informative. Your sense of knowing what to do and when to do it will become nearly palpable.

SWIFT CHANGE

WINTER IS A TIME OF MYSTERY AND MAGIC. SUDDEN CHANGES,
with the speed of a lightning strike, are characteristic in winter. Unexpected death, receiving money that you did not anticipate, the return home of a family member...big changes that happen fast.

To be prepared for such swift, blink of an eye changes—big ones that will have a profound effect on your life—is not an easy task. But there is a practice that can help you become less afraid of sudden gain or loss.

This practice is best done at night in the countryside with someone to accompany you for safety. It is a seemingly simple activity, but not so easy as it sounds.

You and your friend are going to go for a night walk on a country road where there is light traffic. Be sure to put glowing tape, or some kind of tape on your clothing so you are visible to drivers, and choose a road that has a safe shoulder for you to walk along.

The idea is that you are going to count to six as you breathe in while you walk, and six as you breathe out. Your breath needs to be relaxed, not forced, and full. Walking and breathing in this rhythm are the first things to become accustomed to.

Once you have gotten into this rhythm, you are going to soften your gaze, using your peripheral vision only as you walk. Whether you are using a head lamp, a flashlight, the light of the moon, or no light is up to you.

As cars pass, you are going to maintain both the passive, soft, peripheral eyesight and the same rhythm of breath. This will involve resisting the temptation to track the car with your eyes.

Nighttime is a more vulnerable time for us unless we are accustomed to being outdoors. The lights on passing cars are distracting, and tend to draw our attention.

By walking with a steady rhythm and soft gaze, you are teaching your nervous system to relax and stay relaxed, even when the stimulus changes. You are creating a template, a "bottom line" for your body.

When you return from this walk, you will notice how bright all the lights in your house are. You may have a heightened sense of vision and hearing. Try maintaining the same breathing and sight as you enter your home and see if you can maintain this through five minutes of activity.

WHEN THERE IS SUDDEN CHANGE, WE NEED A GROUND TO stand on. Even what we perceive to be positive sudden change can throw us way off balance. There is no bypassing the emotional roller coaster that big shifts bring, but breath and soft eyesight can teach you to have a "go to" internal safe place within which to cocoon and integrate change.

DEEP SLEEP

MOST CREATURES ARE HIBERNATING OR AT LEAST RESTING IN the winter, gathering energy for the next cycle of seasons. Only humans continue to rush around as though the light has not changed; there is no draw to go inward. In fact, the holidays guarantees a ramp up in rushing around.

Sleep is one of the most important processes for good health and renewal of energy, especially deep winter sleep that allows for dreaming.

In many indigenous cultures dreaming, or dreamtime, is considered every bit as important as time awake.

Deep sleep in the winter is unlike sleep in other seasons. Perhaps we are closer to our unconscious selves in winter, or maybe the change in light allows for more information to come through as we sleep. Whatever it is, there is a quality to sleeping in the winter that is especially healing.

95

This practice will involve some effort both outside and inside. To begin, you are going to do your best to claim three late afternoons/evenings for yourself.

Go outside and become very clear on when it is actually dark. In preparation for your three-night practice, bundle up and go outside to witness the last moments of light—not the setting sun, but the final moments before dark. If possible, stay outside in the dark for a few moments.

Inside, you are going to set up a lovely alternative sleeping place for yourself, enclosed, private, comfy, and lit by a light of some sort. This could be a tent, a collection of screens with cloth over them.

Remember when you were little and you loved to build inside forts and special places. This is in the spirit of such a creation.

Only you are going to be in this little sleeping place and No phone, No computer. You can listen to music on a device and you can read. No phone, no computer. No TV.

You will enter this sleeping space after dinner, after dark, and stay there relaxing and reading or listening to music till it's time to go to sleep.

The first night, you will probably be dealing with a head full of "should" and "have tos" that will try to pull you up and out of your refuge, but you will either ignore them or tell yourself they can wait for tomorrow.

You will become aware of the silence of winter. Just allow yourself to relax in the place you have created.

The second night, you will possibly look forward to time spent alone, uninterrupted, reading or listening to music. And your body will enjoy deep sleep.

The third night, because it is the last (unless you make an agreement with yourself or family that you wish to continue sleeping there and having the evening after dinner to yourself) may be slightly unsettled. Maybe. Or, it may be the deepest rest and sleep you have experienced in a long time.

GETTING ENOUGH SLEEP IS NOT ONLY GREAT FOR YOUR general well-being, it improves your outlook on life. You have more energy to expend during the daytime and experiencing the quiet and coziness of an indoor night's deep sleep in winter is very comforting.

Maybe these three days will encourage you to make the majority of your winter evenings more about relaxation, being in tune with the season, and getting the real rest that you need.

DRUMMING

"AH," YOU THINK, "BUT I DON'T OWN A DRUM." DRUMMING is one of the most satisfying winter practices I can offer you in this book, so let's talk about drumming.

I am referring to a Native American style drum. That could be a Taos drum, a Lakota drum...there are numerous styles. If you want a recommendation for a wonderful drum maker who works with horse, elk, moose, and buffalo hides, please be in touch with me on my website and I will give you the best person I know in this country.

Drums can be 15", 18", and larger. The skin of the animal should be one that you feel some connection with. The drums I recommend are made from animal skins that were taken from animals who died naturally or on the road. Personally I don't believe that culled animal hides are ethical, but this is only my belief.

Some people are happy with vegan drums. That is also an option, though the sound is very different.

Why a drum? And why begin in winter?

A drum is a symbol of the earth and all her living beings. We are all related, affecting one another continually in a universe much like a web. Tug on one small part and the whole changes.

We are interwoven, and this is coming more and more into our consciousness, sometimes through positive global connections, other times through the latest pandemic.

A drum is a symbol of this interconnectedness, and it is meant to be an extension of your heart that connects you with the heart of the planet.

Although you may be of any faith, a drum can be another way to express your connection with spirit and all life.

97

Drumming

There are many ways to use a drum, which come with a beater...a mallet to play it with. An animal that gave its life and its spirit is a part of the drum. In that sense, the drum is a living being. You will find that drums have moods...that sometimes they want to be played and other times, not so much!

To get to know your drum, you need to spend time touching it, looking at it from both sides, and finding all the different tones in it. Every drum is unique.

You can begin with a simple heartbeat, ta dum, ta dum...as quietly or as loudly as you like and your surroundings permit.

There are so many ways and reasons to drum. You can sit and drum to connect yourself more to the earth. You can talk with your drum, ask it questions, and then while you play, see what answers come to mind. You will be surprised!

99 Sometimes drumming can send you into an altered state of being, very peaceful, and in tune with the energy around you. Moreover you can drum with a very specific intention for yourself or someone else or a whole group of people. Drumming can be a form of prayer.

In the quiet of winter, you will get to know all the sounds your drum can make. If it gets too cold, warm the hide gently with a hair dryer, or set it near your woodstove. In winter, the sounds will be clear. It is a great time to get to know your drum, so that when springtime comes, you can take it outside and drum to the flowers, and rivers, and sunshine.

Of all the winter practices, getting a drum is most important if the idea calls to you. Give it a try. You will be pleasantly surprised! You don't have to have a sense of rhythm; no musical knowledge is required. Only the willingness to try something new.

A WINTER WALK/TALK

MANY OF US DO NOT GO OUT MUCH IN THE WINTER. TOO
Cold. Too much trouble. Don't have warm clothing.

This walk is to heighten your curiosity and lower your sense of being stuck inside in the winter. Or of winter being "a bad time to go out." Often curiosity is the best remedy for being stuck inside.

If at all possible, whether you live in the city or the country, the best conditions to awaken your winter curiosity are right after a snowfall has stopped.

If you are in the country, you may need snow shoes to walk safely through deep snow, and you will certainly need warm, waterproof clothing. Much of this can be purchased at second hand stores if you don't want to invest in new clothing.

If you are in the city, you will need warm clothing and back streets   100
where you can walk with a minimum of traffic, sirens, and other noise.

First, as you walk (practicing the warming breath), notice the shape of things. Notice how the snow redefines contours, softens, highlights, and transforms all shapes, natural and manmade.

Notice the muting of sound, the quiet after a fresh snow.

If you are in a city, use all your senses to be aware of how the snow has altered the simplest of things. Where has it created interesting "hats" on fire hydrants? What is covered that is usually visible? Does the air smell different? Do you hear fewer vehicles? Are any birds singing after the snow? Are there footprints of others who have ventured out, or are you making the first tracks along a street? Has your sense of time changed? How does it feel to touch newly fallen snow?

Is there anywhere to make a snowman/woman/sculpture?

If you are in the countryside, do you see any deer, mouse, birdwing markings in the snow? Were any other creatures on the move while you were sitting comfortably in your house?

Look at the shapes of trees, how their trunks bow with the weight of the snow, how their limbs are reshaped by the brightness against the bark. Are there any red berries to be found, any color to contrast the white?

Can you be with the stillness and quiet even though you are moving? Do you remember how snow is created? Is there any urge to play...throw snowballs, make a snow angel?

If the sun is out, can you see the rainbow sparkles on the snow? Can you see the shape of snow on rocks if you are near a stream? Are there icicles? Look at all the forms of water, flowing, frozen, in between.

If you are near a river, can you hear the ice breaking under the water? Is there a place where an edge is created between flowing water and ice?

As you walk, just stay curious and present. About 20 minutes to an hour is great, however long you can remain warm and curious.

THE BENEFITS OF OBSERVING THE WONDERS OF WINTER ARE many. Winter no longer becomes this season to avoid going out into. Winter has incredible beauty and is a great shapeshifter. Your health will improve by bundling up and going out and moving, or by the warm dinner you make, or hot chocolate you drink upon returning to your home which will taste twice as good.

LONG EXHALE

OF HIBERNATING BEAR

UNDER ICICLE LIGHT

OF WOLF MOON,

LANDSCAPE RESHAPED,

SNOW BLANKET

102

CAPTURED FIRE

IN WOODSTOVE HEART.

—Rebecca Singer

103

Earth Practices

I HOPE YOU HAVE TRIED SOME, IF NOT ALL, OF THESE PRAC-
TICES. I HOPE YOU HAVE A NEW CONNECTION WITH EACH
SEASON, AND THAT THIS IS A BOOK YOU WILL BRING ALONG
WITH YOU THROUGHOUT THE YEARS.

Practices mean just that. In the same way you practice a piano to learn to play, or basketball to become adept, you can return to this book each season.

Perhaps the reality of learning from a rock or tree or river is not so unusual now.

The seasons reflect the cyclical nature of life, the turning from one time of year to another. They call us to listen, look, observe, and learn. There is a natural rhythm just waiting for you to tune into each season, changes of light, temperature, and growth.

These external seasons that repeat each year reflect the seasons of your life. I hope that after doing the practices in this book, you have a tactile, kinetic understanding of this relationship. That every season calls to you. That you are not only willing, but happy to go outdoors any time of year to appreciate, observe, and be grateful for the wonders that will present themselves to you, both external and internal.

If you have deepened your appreciation for the natural world, learned that you are one of many life forms in it, and come to see yourself as a part of a wondrous whole, then this little book has served you well.

Good work! Time well spent. You have ventured out to go inward. Nature, like us, loves to be appreciated. To be noticed. May your seasons flow, and may you stand in the direction of the flow, willing, curious, and welcomed.

.

ABOUT THE AUTHOR

RECOGNIZED AS A HEALER BY THE INDIGENOUS TRIBES PEOPLE of the Costa Rican rainforest and the Reindeer People of Mongolia, internationally known shaman Rebecca Singer is a modern embodiment of ancient healing wisdom.

She is author of "Singing into Bone," stories of her experiences in both other realms and other countries, including her life in Costa Rica and living with The Reindeer People in Mongolia. Her unusual path as a healer is unveiled in stories of adventure and daily life.

Rebecca has been teaching people of many nationalities and ages Earth Practices, both individually and through workshops throughout the USA, in Canada, Costa Rica, and now in New York near Woodstock where she, her husband, two dogs, cat, and rabbit reside.

Rebecca has been published in *Shaman's Hoop* and *The Journal of Contemporary Shamanism*. She continues to offer seasonal teachings online, in person healing as well as online sessions. Her classes available through her website.

You can find her at **www.shamanicenergy.com**

ALSO BY REBECCA SINGER

SINGING into BONE

STORIES of VISION and HEALING

by Rebecca Singer

Found wherever books are sold.